SITUATIONS GATHERED

◇

Hesham Salama

authorHOUSE®

AuthorHouse™
1663 Liberty Drive, Suite 200
Bloomington, IN 47403
www.authorhouse.com
Phone: 1-800-839-8640

First published by AuthorHouse   7/23/2008

ISBN: 978-1-4389-0613-3 (sc)

Printed in the United States of America
Bloomington, Indiana

This book is printed on acid-free paper.

I like to dedicate this book to my professor and mentor, Dr. Marvin V. Anthony and my professor, Dr. Nancy Arduengo who taught me a great deal about leadership, writing, and self-expression. I also dedicate it to all my colleagues and friends who supported and encouraged me after reading my first book, *Leave People Alone* as well as all my dear readers.

INTRODUCTION

Once upon a time, there was a leader who scared his people to win the presidential elections. He used September 11, 2001 to be reelected. He did not care how he wins, whether he is being honest or not, whether his legacy will continue flourishing or not. He accused his rival to be a "flip flopper." He is always successful in using new expressions and titles to describe others, as well as himself. That is the "decider" in chief.

Of course, everybody knows that the decider in chief is President George W. Bush. President Bush decided to go to war in Iraq saying Iraq had weapons of mass destructions. In fact, his policy is the destruction itself. He destructed many human lives of Americans, Iraqis, and others. He caused others to be amputated, disfigured, and orphaned. How in the world can he fix all the damage he had done? Why did those innocents have to pay for his cruelty?

Besides the cruelty that resulted from war actions in Iraq, there is another cruelty that is resulted from the failure policy of President Bush. People cannot afford eating properly like before. They do not drive as much as before and they still suffer. People can hardly afford their kids' school expenses. They cannot buy them proper meals or even snacks to eat during the school day. Who in the world had imagined America will experience such miserable situations one day?! Nobody in the world had such a thought at all. Why did those situations occur? Those situations are a combination of President Bush and his administration failures and wickedness. With President Bush, his administration, their intelligence leaders, and most important of all; the triangle of Dick Cheney, Donald Rumsfeld, and Condoleezza Rice, situations are gathered.

THE BEGINNING

One day, while working in my part time job in that pizza restaurant in Depo Town, a conversation took place between Bashar, the owner then and some of the workers. In fact, I was just a worker and a listener. I listened attentively while making a pizza for an order. The conversation was about who was going to be a better president, Bush or Al Gore.

Bashar supported Al Gore. Another worker named Hakim supported Bush. He said "Bush is the Arab's friend." I thought about that sentence I heard from Hakim because I had heard it so many times in the previous few days. I also heard it from my sister. My sister Aida was in California to have her Certified Public Accountant (CPA) exam. That was the only way she could have such an exam as it was just available in the United States. She decided to come and visit me in Michigan before going back home to Cairo.

Aida also told me that Bush was supported by most of the Arab people in America and everyone knows he is a real friend of Arabs. I was more than surprised to hear that from Aida too. Another guy who is a friend named Ahmed Yehia supported Bush and said he is a good and intelligent person who will make a good leader. I never felt that Bush will be a good president and I was always in the favor of Al Gore.

I heard many times that Republicans are completely different from Democrats. As I heard and as I recollected my memory about both Republicans and Democrats, Republicans were always in favor of wars and power. Democrats proved to be considerate people who preferred peaceful solutions. Democrats cared more about the people. They were not after making legacies out of themselves at the expense of the innocent people.

President Bush excelled all the expectations. The Arabs' friend became their enemy. The people who helped a great deal electing him became his victims. Those of the Arabs who were not hurt physically by his wicked actions became terrorists in his eyes. He announced mobilization against them.

Hakim, my Iraqi coworker who said Bush is our friend became totally silent that day when Bush bombed Iraq. This was a while before September 11, 2001. The air strike against Iraq then was because of the same false pretences of the weapons of mass destruction (WMD). When Hakim talked, he said, "How come the one who was said to be our friend, the person we elected, trusted, and loved does that to us? I cannot believe it."

Hakim could not believe it but I could. I could because I know he was not a good politician. I knew he was going to seek his dad's advice in everything. I knew he will not be his own decision-maker. I knew it. In fact, during the same days, I talked with my friend Mahdi Huwio about Bush. I told Mahdi that I had a feeling that Al Gore would make a better president because of the eight years he spent as vice president and because of the flourishing era of the Clinton-Gore administration. Mahdi said Bush can be successful too because of his father's past experience as president.

THE FLORIDA COUNT

Too many discussions took place about the Florida count. Many people said Governor Jeb Bush faked the results of Florida for the sake of his brother. Whether it is true or not, I have never felt comfortable towards Bush. I have never felt he will respect all the other races, especially Arabs. I knew the rulers' words and actions affect the actions of their people towards others very much. I knew it was not going to be a good presidency. All my friends told me I was wrong. I told them I hope they were right. It did not really matter if I was right or wrong. I was more than worried about the results of him being elected as president.

I used to watch Bush-Cheney and Gore-Lieberman press conferences in the news and what they said about each others. It was confusing as it was hard to tell who the best was. It was all just guesses and wishes. I also watched the confrontation between Senator John McCain and Governor George W. Bush of Texas in Larry King Live and how senator McCain told Bush he should be ashamed of saying something negative about him.

Believe it or not, I never believed anything Bush said. Maybe Bush had been a successful politician when he was the Texas Governor. However, I knew some Texans who said he did not care very much about the healthcare of the poor people and that he always escaped answering hard questions with a combination of intelligence and diplomacy. That is why I think a successful politician does not always make a successful president or leader.

Hence, the Florida count was the beginning of the real disaster of America and the Universe. No matter how Bush and Cheney won the elections, they brought a great deal of misery and dissatisfaction to the earth. They thought they were going to make new history for new Victorians represented by both of them besides other major figures in their administration.

THE BUSH ADMINISTRATION AND CRITICISM

The Bush administration always received any kind of criticism or advice with indifference and contempt. For example, every time someone said that administration was wrong about any issue or decision, Vice President Dick Cheney always made fun of him or her. He never took that advice with consideration or respect. I cannot tell or understand why he always had such an attitude. Anyone can make mistakes. Why was it always so hard for him to admit he or the administration were wrong? The president was not different either. Maybe they had a deal before starting their administration always to act in such a way.

During the first few days of the war against Iraq, Vice President Cheney made fun of the comments of the retired military personnel who criticized the style used in the Iraqi war. He laughed sarcastically saying those were comments coming from "Retired Generals embedded in TV studios." Maybe because he said and imagined the ***mission*** was going to be ***accomplished*** sooner. He forgot that those retired Generals and military staff who are very experienced militarily like him. Maybe he was not aware that all of them had to take important field actions and decisions during their military careers and such experiences cannot be forgotten.

Unfortunately, President Bush used the support he got from Americans and others all over the world in a bad way. He used that support pretending he was going to eradicate terrorism, which of course, all of us wanted with him. He increased terrorism and terrorists. He helped overspreading poverty, crime, and lack of discipline. He caused many disasters directly and indirectly.

THAT IS TOTALLY FALSE

During one of their presidential debates, Bush interrupted Al Gore about a statement he made telling him, "Wait! Wait! That is totally false." If someone does not know the president, he would say, "Oh yeah! That is the right person to choose. His statements are all correct. He is a man of his word. He never gives a false statement."

Now, everyone can tell that President Bush's State of the Union Speech in 2003 before the Iraq war was *"totally false."* No single word was correct in your glorious and fascinating speech Mr. president. You deceived the whole world. You lied to your own people. You made republicans and democrats mobilize their effort to support you. If you were correct, nobody would have dared to blame you. You were wrong because you used terrorism and other harsh words to describe other people. You said you were going on and nothing was going to stop your *"Crusades."* You are the one who made yourself a crusader.

Who was false then; Al Gore or you, Mr. President? Al Gore was explaining his policy and how he was going to do his best to please the people and satisfy their financial and medical needs and you accused him of lying? We never saw that. We saw your policy and how you were going to do better than Al Gore, did you?

I think you never did. People are suffering financially, medically, and emotionally because of the great deal of stress they are suffering from now. This suffering is due to lack of jobs, funds, and more important, lack of sufficient policies. The policy of your administration is causing people to experience foreclosure. People are losing their houses because of you and politicians who act the same way like you.

THE BUSH SUPPORTERS

I s it possible that the people, who supported President Bush, especially before the second term of his presidency, still believe they were right? Everything is possible now. Some people still find excuses for President Bush by saying what is happening now in terms of gas prices is a natural result because people are consuming a lot of oil. What about the other oil, which is being burned everyday in Iraq? Doesn't that affect too? Who was the reason behind that whole Iraqi swamp and mess? Is it President Bush and his administration or someone else? Do you guys think all the situations were just gathered; against President Bush and his administration?

You thought President Bush was going to protect you, did he? Did he protect you from the unreasonable high prices of food and gas? Did he make America safer? Did he make you more comfortable? Perhaps, he did but how, unless you are a multi millionaire, and you do not experience the sufferings of the poor, miserable people.

Look at the situations of just the American people in general and tell me how he could make America better. You supported him and defied the others who told you he is not working for your sake. How did he benefit you? Do you expect any coming president will be able to fix that mess very soon unless he owns Aladdin's magic lamp?

However, I hope you have learned a lesson from your mistake. Although I do not think any coming president will be able to make life more glorious and vivid soon, it is still wise to choose the right person. For example, look at the John McCain's vision towards Iraq and the one hundred year plan he suggested. If you say he might change his mind, he may cut the one hundred years into a 90 or 85 year plan, which in turn, will make you no good at all; neither you, your sons and daughters, or even your grandchildren.

THE CURRENT TIME

Look at the miserable era we are living at the moment and how many people use begging, stealing, robbing, and lying to get away with anything. Situations are gathered here too. I never try to find any excuses for people's wicked actions. However, many people go astray when things do not go well for them.

I will talk about myself here, and please allow me to do that, just to clarify the situation. It is not my habit to talk about myself. I have a master's degree and working on my doctorate degree, almost half way. The best job I could find in the United States, which I can say, it might be related a little bit to my degrees and certificate is a substitute teacher. I know everyone can imagine how that job goes. There was a TV commercial about a kind of aspirin asking, "What do you do for a living? Are you a substitute teacher? What a big headache!" I do agree completely with that statement. You can imagine if you are familiar with the Ypsilanti, Ann Arbor, Detroit, and Dearborn areas, how it is to be called to work in a school in Dear Born and you live in Ann Arbor. You go there and the people in charge of that school send you back home, apologize to you because the original teacher had shown up. How would you feel then? Do you see my point, and how gas prices affects people's lives, attitudes, feeling, living, and everything? How do most of the people who do not have a satisfactory job that pays a salary, and I mean ***salary***, not a regular hourly job, feel stressed and disappointed? Are situations gathered here or not? Why were such bad situations gathered? Is it a mere chance? Of course not, it is one of the simplest results of the failure of President Bush and his policy.

It is not about me

Giving the previous example, it is not my intention to comment on my jobs or my life. The example can applied on simple people's lives. If I had to drive a long distance from Ann Arbor to Dear Born or Detroit and come back, consider the amount of gas I had to consume. Look how much it was worse when I went but did not work and was just sent back home, driving both ways, for nothing with such high cost of living and prices that most of the people can hardly afford at this time.

It is about the poor and helpless people. My situation might be much better than many others. Thank God for everything. Thank God also that many people who suffer from those situations and worse are still honest and nice. However, a large number of people are deviating. Too many of them chose the wrong direction. They cannot see the right way and find themselves excuses for committing crimes and theft.

No, my friends; crime never pays. You might end up dead or go to prison for the rest of your life. In addition to yourselves, you should still think about others whom you kill, injure, steal, or hurt in any way.

Those people you hurt or think recklessly about hurting are suffering from the same bad situations like you, if not worse than you. You need to leave those people alone if you cannot help them, don't hurt them; don't steal their money or the money of the people they work for? If you feel helpless, don't lose your mind. Be wise, otherwise, you deserve anything that happens to you, and blame yourselves before blaming others. We all know that bad situations are gathered. All what we can do is to advise one another, to help if we can or not to attack others who are suffering from the same situations.

My other jobs

D ue to all the circumstances I explained about myself, I work as a cashier in some gas stations. Everyone can tell how that job can be hard sometimes for cashiers, especially in gas stations. Many customers take it for granted that it is more than all right for them to be rude, mean, ugly, and lousy to gas stations' cashiers. Some of those customers really consider it a fact. They see those cashiers to be their slaves or that individual cashier in front of them to be the slave mummy or daddy had bought for them to serve and get insulted and humiliated by them.

Let me give you some examples of what I experience. One of the gas stations does not have a public rest room. I have hard times from the owners and the customers because of that rest room issue. The owners blame me if I once try to be nice and give the key to a customer and treat me like a little schoolboy although I am older than the oldest of them. Some of the customers express their misery and dissatisfaction with me. I explain to them that I am a worker and I am not happy with that either but who do you talk to? You talk to people who look down on you and are just ready to insult you. What can you do about it? Either be patient or lose your job and find someone to support you.

Someday, I lost patience because of such practices especially from the owners. A coworker of mine who knows me very well and knows everything about me and my life said to me, "You have to be patient. People who are university graduates cannot find jobs." I said to him, "What do you think of me?" Don't you know I am a university graduate too, and moreover I have a graduate diploma and a Master's degree?"

However, I can still understand what he meant as this is what kept me doing such kind of jobs. I am not ashamed to do any kind of job. To the contrary, a gas station cashier is a good and honest job. I am just trying to figure out why people act this way with gas stations' cashiers? Is it a hobby or something else?

Besides having that hobby of humiliating people, I was told that most of the people are upset and stressed because of the high gas and food prices. People cannot figure out how they will continue living this way and for how long they can do it. I can understand that. Therefore, some of them blame the cashier and increase the misery he or she (mostly he) already has. Therefore, situations are gathered here too. Such wicked situations, which resulted from the Bush-Cheney administration and their reckless policies and agenda influence the way people are dealing with one another nowadays. That is why I am telling the majority of Americans who voted for Bush and Cheney, "Here you are guys! I hope you are enjoying your wise choice."

We Are Humans

Why are people getting meaner, nastier, uglier, and lousier every day? Conditions, economics, circumstances, politics, all these can be good excuses. The question is: Why do they have to show their anger or use it against people who have nothing to do with their misery? We are all miserable. For instance, working as a cashier, if I make a mistake and correct it, customers are still so rude. I am in my job to make a living, not to get insulted or humiliated.

What is the end of all that? Too much is going on. Deceptions from people who use religion and ethics to rob me, and lack of appreciation all over, are occurring all the time. What do you think of a person who waits until I put the money in the cash register and then pretends he or she gave me a 20 dollar bill instead of 10? And if I am wrong, I correct the mistake but I have to get a dirty look from his or her highness and majesty.

Those people think they live in heaven. It is a human world. It is always subject to mistakes. Because I know very well the reality of our world, I am forced to expect the worst before the best. I am losing the least amount of faith I had in humans and humanity. I love the whole world but the world is cruel. The world is exactly like the fish in the sea, the bigger fishes eat the smaller ones.

DID YOU SPIT IN MY FOOD OR DRINK?

According to my memory, I watched that in an American TV show. I think it is "Roots", in which a lady spit in the water she gave to an old man she used to know when they were both children. She felt a great deal of satisfaction after that.

I was shocked the first time someone asked me not to spit in his food when he ordered food from the pizza restaurant I worked at. I was very offended. It was on the phone. I did not comment first then he repeated the request for me not to spit in his food.

The same thing occurred again 10 years later in another pizza restaurant I worked for in Ann Arbor. I also got offended because I forgot about the first time. I remembered all that stupidity today. A customer bought an ice tea can. After paying, he opened it and drank a little talking to his friend. He forgot his ice tea on my counter and came back to me after a few minutes. I gave it to him. He said, "You did not spit in my ice tea, did you?" I was shocked as there is a long gap between the three times those three stupid, mean, and rude customers asked me that. I said, "No." He said to me again, "Are you sure you did not?" I said to him, "If I was to spit in your ice tea, I would not keep it for you as I do not care about you then. I would just throw it away;" **peculiar people and peculiar situations.**

BEHIND THE SCENES

On Wednesday June 19, 2008, an assault and robbery in Dairy Mart, Grove road Ypsilanti took place at 3:30 a.m. I got assaulted, hit on my head so many times, threatened to be killed, insulted, and humiliated by two idiots, two useless people who just want an easy life, who steal others' money and effort to spend them on drugs, women, or any useless source. Such trivial people should get capital punishment. I wish there were capital punishment in Michigan so such stupid people get it and become an example to those idiots who think about acting in such a violent manner. This capital punishment will be a protection for a whole society. It will teach people to become useful. It will let them know that "every action has a reaction." If one of those cowards knows he was going to get a death sentence, he will reconsider a million time before he or she does it. If there is no consideration or reconsideration, he or she will deserve whatever he or she gets. I wish Michigan officials impose the death penalty. It is a protection for people, whether those people are good or bad. Some bad people might become good citizens. If not, and they still think about robbery, they might not combine it with violence.

Innocent people pay the price too expensive for nothing they have done except for being honest. A cashier who bleeds from his head and find a reckless and mean customer enter the station, asking him to sell him cigarettes, how should he feel? The customer did not move to do something about his bleeding and wanted cigarettes. Can people be mean to that extent?!

It is me, the cashier who bled from his head, and did not know until the two armed and masked robbers left him drowning in his blood? What did I do? What did the owner of the gas station do to pay for the expenses of my hospital besides the money he already lost in such a robbery? Why do we pay the price? I blame the laws. I know someone has to pay but it should not be us. It should be the criminals. These criminals and people like them should be brought to justice. They should be punished properly. They should never get out of prison. Why will they go out? They have to be locked up for life. They should not continue their corruption; stealing, robbing, and terrorizing others.

People need to live in peace, which is impossible to achieve with such kind of valueless creatures. In fact, they are not worth to be called creatures. Sometimes, people use the word dog or donkey to insult and humiliate others. This nomination is not fair at all. Dogs and donkeys are faithful and honest. They do not deceive or cheat. They do not hurt people unless people start hurting them.

What are those people who are ready to kill for a dollar? Where did they come from? Who taught them? Did nobody bring them up or teach them that it is important to work to make a living? How come do they just go and steal and moreover combine their stealing with killing?

Some years ago, a guy from Yemen named Saleh, was working in his midnight shift in a gas station. An idiot came and robbed him. He ended up killing Saleh, stealing his car, driving from this gas station in Ann Arbor to Detroit, invading a second gas station, ordered the workers under the threat of his gun to take off the safe from its place, and put it in the stolen car of Saleh. While leaving, he told them, "You have to thank me because I did not kill you." How great is that? His Excellency thinks he is the God who takes people's life or give it to them.

I wish the people who oppose the death penalty reconsider. Look how those people act. Those criminals are cowards' guys. A large number of them will not do what they do in case of imposing the death penalty. Ask me how the two robbers who robbed and injured me were scared that anyone would show up at the station. If I was sure the gun they had is not a real one, which I do not know yet and do not know if I will ever know about that or not, I would have defended myself much better. Those two persons are the cowards, whom I had never seen like before in my whole life.

What do you guys think of a person who kills? If he or she finds that a human life of a human is worthless, why do you defend him or her? You are encouraging others to do the same thing. You are not helping your society. You are damaging it. Just think about it guys if it happens, God Forbids, to a loved one of yours, who gets killed by one of those idiots.

I know some people will say his or her execution is not going to bring back my loved one. I agree but don't you think it might happen to another loved one of yours, or even to you? What guarantee do you have that it will never happen to you?

I did not get killed but I got injured. They could have killed me by any means, even if the gun they had was not a real one. Don't you think they could have done it? At that time, I thought it might be the very last moment in my life. Imagine guys being a cashier in a store by yourself, and you find two masked persons attacking you, cursing you with words and sentences that are improper at all. Do you deserve that? I am sure you do not.

Let's take an action, and urge the authorities to impose the death penalty in Michigan. Let's do something. Let's not stay silent for the rest of our lives. Let's move. Let's go on but we need to go on positively, not negatively. I know as I said in previous chapters of this book that bad situations are gathered. That is why actions must be taken to fix everything. Society will not be improved with high crime rates. Those gathered situations make honest people like you and me work harder and try to find two or three jobs in order to make a living. It is not fair for all of us, I know, as we can hardly find time for any pleasure or amusement. Moreover, we can hardly rest or sleep. Therefore, we do not want our miserable lives to become much worse by being killed, attacked, or threatened by such criminals.

Different Laws for Different Circumstances and Places

I remember that President Bush was met with demonstrations in Europe, particularly in Spain, because of applying the death penalty in some American states. I have a great deal of respect for the European opinion. However, I believe the circumstances and the situations of the state and the place impose a certain criteria for whether to apply a certain law or judgment. It is thoughtful to cancel the death penalty in a state or country that does not suffer from high crime rates but what should happen if crimes are increasing every day? The person who murders another intentionally will not mind murdering others. It becomes a regular habit for them.

I think most of the American states now, and Michigan in particular, need to reconsider and implement new laws that protect the innocent people from those who know nothing about honesty or respect of human life and dignity. The current financial situations are helping doing that. What I am saying and repeating is: Those situations are gathered against me, you, and those criminals. Therefore, such criminals have no excuse to attack us. We already have more than enough. If we cannot get help to improve our deteriorating conditions, we deserve, at least, to be left alone.

I hope this presidency and administration can do something to protect us. They helped us to feel helpless and uncomfortable. Now, it is their turn, with the approach of the end of their glorious era to do something that might decrease our pain. Will they do anything? I really doubt it. They might accomplish their mission, making us more tired, angry, and upset; fed up from them and their policies.

I was always against carrying guns. Now, I want to get one to defend myself in case I have to. If the two criminals who attacked me with the back of a gun on my head carried a gun, why shouldn't I have one with which I would have shot both of them as soon as I saw them entering the store with their masks and gun? Can anyone blame me then? If people find excuses for thieves, why won't they find one for me when I kill or injure a criminal for self-defense?

Have those two criminals and similar people learned anything in their lives? I do not think so, even if they were graduated from schools and universities. Nobody has taught them the meanings of ethics, work, respect, or cooperation. Of course, the two criminals have learned to cooperate and coordinate together to steal, rob, kill, and injure. They cooperated and coordinated as they attacked me; one was watching the road while the other was doing a good job threatening, pushing, and hitting me.

What is the Choice?

hat do you think a better choice should have been? Staying as a substitute teacher with those gas prices, no matter how many times I go to the assigned school and then being sent home? Was it good to go preparing myself to work for a certain teacher of a certain class then I find them assigning and scheduling me with a different class of a different grade and different subjects?

Was it a better choice to stay in the gas stations having issues with the owners and customers about why we did not have a public restroom and how that was improper for most of them? Is it good when a customer stops another who bought his stuff after giving me a bunch of change saying keep the rest of that change, to ask him why he gave me too much money? Believe me; I have never expected to experience any of those single situations in my whole life. That customer who stopped the other about the too much change he gave me had an excellent excuse. Her excuse was that she needed that change more than me and that is why she should get it. Do you know what happened then? That customer told me to give her the extra change which was more than ok with me.

I gave her the rest of the change and she yelled at me saying it was more than what I am giving her. I could not help it and shouted back at her telling her it was none of her business, in the first place, interfering between me and the other customer, to tell him he gave me too much money and justifying that telling me she needed that change.

Anyway, her way of getting some change was still better than the one of the robbers. The main question is: Why do we see such strange situations nowadays more than any time before? Why are many people ready to do anything to get some money, even less than a dollar? Why are people becoming ruder than any other time ever? Is it because of all the current situations that are gathered as a result of the mistakes of the Bush administration?

CASH OR CREDIT

Nowadays, people are getting upset and angry about what many gas stations' owners are doing. Some of the gas stations are charging the customers who pay for gas by credit some cents more than when they pay by cash. The owners of the stations say they lose money and they have to do such a thing so as to decrease their loss due to the high gas prices. Gas stations' owners always say their profit usually comes from the goods such as candy, gums, and other groceries they sell inside their stores and hardly any from the gas.

The difference in prices between cash and credit started with few cents like 3 or 4 cents. By the time of writing these lines, the difference reached more than 15 cents in some stations. I think both owners and customers have their excuses to be upset. They both put the cashier as usual in the middle and let him or her deal with the cruelty of some of the customers.

Let me tell you about one of the exciting situations that happened to me. A lady who is a regular customer came to buy gas as usual. She stood in front of me for more than 10 minutes thinking whether to pay cash or credit. That was at the first few days of applying that different prices system between cash and credit. Finally, she decided to pay by credit. She tried three cards and none of them worked. I was very patient as it is always my habit with my customers and all the people I meet and deal with in general.

Her fourth card worked and she paid by her credit card to get $ 50.00 worth of gas in her van. She came back to me in a minute. She started murmuring saying that is dishonest, cheating…etc. She said, "Give me my money back." Because that customer paid inside the station and not at the pump, her card had to be charged that amount of $50.00 according to the credit card system in that station and many other ones. I told her that she should get her refund automatically in about 24 hours, and this is how the system works.

She blocked the way of the other customers and told me she was not going to leave unless I give her a refund back. She stood in front of me for more than one hour insulting me and accusing me of stealing her $50.00. I told her I hoped she would come back after finding out she was wrong to apologize but she never did.

During that hour, I called the owners and told them about the situation. They refused to talk to her and told me to deal with her myself. One of them told me just to tell her to come tomorrow to meet the owner. I did before and after he told me that so many times but he was trying to get away from any headaches as long as there is some other person who was going to take it, whether he likes it or not, because he works for him. What a great thing to do! Maybe it is an honor but I do not know yet.

That customer ended up calling the police for me. The owner called back after a while and I told him about that police issue. He advised me to explain the situation to the police, which of course I did not need his valuable advice about. The police came, took my driver's license and wrote down my information, which was still more than all right with the owners. Look at the way my situations are gathered. Having to work to make a living can be so humiliating. However, I do not choose the easy way and go to steal and rob people like the two thieves I told you about before. We work hard and do the best of our best, and our situations are still deteriorating every day. What can we do to conquer those gathered situations?

The Money Value

Nowadays, it is hard to feel we achieved something with any amount of money we get. Money is losing its value. Just think about what you can buy with money now and how much you need to make your dreams come true. You need millions and maybe billions. Conditions were different only a few years ago. You could have bought something valuable with a reasonable amount of money.

If you double the same amount of money now, can you buy a property? Can you do it paying the entire amount at one time? How many people can do that at our current time? And if you can buy something valuable, how many years will you be in debt, cutting your expenses and still finds yourself unable to make a balance between your daily needs and your savings to pay your debt? How ridiculous is that?!

We are in the age of suffering   . We have to pay the price of the falsehood of the leaders who deceive us. We have to tolerate the leaders' wickedness and lying when they accuse others of falsehood and they are the falsehood itself, if not worse as they excel any falsehood in the world. Those leaders are letting us down every day. They are giving us a very good lip service and nothing else. Where in the world can people cash their sweet promises? People might cash them from the bank of *Happy Dreams* or the financial institution of *Good Wishes*. Maybe the same leaders satisfy our curiosity with another good lip service.

THE GOOD LIP SERVICE ADMINISTRATION

The administration started its two terms with wonderful promises for a better future accusing the first rival of saying false statements and the second one with being a flip flopper. People are very good at believing the one who lies to them. They look at the one who is good at decorating sentences and words and adore him or her. Why do people like the person who lies to them? How in the world can people vote for a second time after four years of falsehood, bad economy, deterioration, spying, lying, and spoiling everything nationally and internationally for the same person and the same administration that showed them all that?

I know that too many women voted for Bush because they believed him to be stronger and he was going to protect them. Those same women come to me in my job and direct their anger and dissatisfaction at me because of the terrible gas prices. Those women should turn their anger against themselves and their wonderful choice. Blame yourselves ladies before blaming me. I used to tell them I am just worker, not an owner or even a manager. Why do you do something wrong and then you expect others to tolerate your attitude?

I am not just saying it is only women who voted for Bush but lots of men too and some of them still do the same thing. I also tell those men who voted for Bush to blame themselves first before blaming me or any other helpless person like me who is very dissatisfied like them with what is happening at the moment. I used to explain to people that my job is just a cashier to make a living but believe me; I got tired of such explanations. Why do I have to explain? They know the answer pretty well. They do not need my response. They just need someone to pour their wrath at.

Hold Your Horses

Needing to pour her wrath at someone, let me go back to the issue of the same lady who accused me of stealing her $50.00 from her credit card account. As you have read, my dear readers, she called the police for me after arguing with me for one hour. After all my explanations to her, as well as my perplexity between her and the owner of the business, she could not hold her horses. After finally God responded to my prayers and let her get a little away from my counter, she stood there on her phone telling the police, "The man there charged me and refuse to give me my money back."

The police came and stood with her outside listening to her angry side of the story. A nice regular customer came and told me that somebody must be in trouble as it seems this lady over there called the police for him. I told her that was me, the person in trouble. She wanted to know why as she sees me all the time. I told her the reason. She said that was not fair and everyone now knows how the credit card systems work. She also added that the angry lady must be just upset because of the unreasonable prices we are all suffering from.

I used to see the angry lady at least about twice a week. That incident took place about three weeks ago and I have not seen her since then. I doubt that she did not show up because she is ashamed of herself because of her accusations and actions. She could have come to apologize if she really felt that way. Anyway, I do not expect any apologies or anything from her. There is an old proverb that says, "If you do not feel ashamed of your actions, do whatever you want."

The issue is we feel upset when an action like that occurs from a person we think has some respect and appreciation towards us. It is really a shock when we respect someone very much, then he or she comes and surprises us with such false accusations, which are baseless. It is never right to let our inner feelings interfere with our relations and actions with others who did not hurt us. I trusted and respected that lady very much but she let me down with her insults and actions. That was not it. She added to all what she had done by shouting at me in front of the two policemen after all the explanations I gave her before and after the coming of the police.

Moreover, if I am a thief who steals her money, shouldn't I be scared when she first threatened to call the police for me? Are people losing their minds nowadays? Can't people think properly any more? Besides, if she is so careful like that, there is a big clear sign outside saying the price of gas with cash and underneath it, the price with credit was written and posted.

Let me tell you something funnier. Another day, another lady came and filled up her car tank. She opened the door of her car, started it, and started moving. I had to run after her because I have to pay for any drive off from my own pocket. I did not accuse her of stealing or running away or anything like that. I just knocked at her door. She stopped and said to me, "What is your problem?" I said, "I have no problem. You forgot to pay for your gas." She said to me, "Did I ever run away from you." I said no, and I had to go inside as there were other customers waiting for me.

She then came and paid. After paying, she kept standing in front of me and said she needed my boss. I called him for her thinking she wanted him for another issue. She wanted to complain to him about me. How in the world do those people think?! I never thought she is going to run away. To be honest, I did not apologize because I was doing my job and I did nothing wrong. How can I prove to her when she comes in the following time, if I ever see her again, that she did not pay then? She would never believe me and that was my point. I can just say two famous sentence an old friend and colleague of mine used to say very often: "God helps us! We suffer."

TV Commercials and Real Life

Do you remember the TV commercial of that lady who was working in a fast food restaurant? A customer was blaming her for not putting the stuff she needs on her sandwiches and gave her a good lecture? This really happens in real life most of the time. That is why I do not blame that cashier girl who was telling herself silently that she deserved better than that.

I tell myself the same sentence sometimes. It last happened to me the same day after that angry credit lady left me, and almost all the other customers knew that police officer and car was there for me. The worst thing is that many people do not act well or even change their attitude when they see someone in such a situation. They also come to have fun and entertain themselves at the expense of another person who is already suffering.

Three other ladies came one after the other. Every one of them took her turn accusing me of misleading, deception, stealing, taking advantage of people. I combined all their accusation to you guys so you do not feel bored. As it is always my habit again, I was patient. I explained the situation to them and told them I already had a problem about what they were talking about and that police car was there for me. To my surprise, they all said they knew that already. So, why then were you coming to me with new problems?!

At that point, I got sick of everything. I said to them, "Listen ladies! If you have a problem, talk to the owner about it." They all asked where my owner was. I answered that he was at home and they needed to call or come to him the following day. Two of them repeated their accusations. One left and came back to ask for a business card to call him. Then, she came with a new question; "Is debit considered like cash or credit." I answered it was considered credit. She said that was stealing again and wondered why. I said to her, "You already got the business card. Call the owner or come to talk to him tomorrow."

I know the owner does not like the way I acted. I did nothing wrong but I mean he does not like me to tell customers to talk to him and he is the owner as he wants me to solve all the problems myself. It is more than ok to get insulted, humiliated, yelled at or anything you can imagine. I work for him and that is the situation with many business owners who think they bought the people with the money they pay them. They forget they pay them because they serve them and take care of their business.

In such situations, I always pray God and ask for his help. Can you imagine many customers know the owner personally and they still come to me and other cashiers complaining about business situations and issues they do not like? They act towards me and other cashiers in a very mean way and then go back and talk to the owner and smile to him in a very friendly way? Isn't that ridiculous?! Do you see how all the bad situations are gathered? Bad administration, thoughtless customers, inconsiderate owners…etc, all are gathered to torment us. Again, like what my friend Magdy used to say, "God help us! We suffer."

VERY PROUD PEOPLE

Why do many people like to be so proud? It is not bad for a person to be proud of himself, herself, or loved ones. What I mean here is the other kind of pride. Why do some people are too proud to say they made a mistake? We are all humans and nobody is perfect. Everyone knows that. I am saying that because I might find someone like my friend Dr. John Green saying to me, "Everybody knows that and you are adding nothing new." I say to him, "Ok John! You made your point clear and I still respect your opinions."

I am saying that here because, as you already know my dear readers, I am talking about the issue of reelecting President George W. Bush. Why many of you guys are unable to admit the truth and say you made a terrible mistake. Others like John have never voted at all, saying he does not vote as his vote will not change anything. That is a very negative thing to say Dr. John Green.

If you start by yourself, you and many others, you will change a lot. Stop that negative attitude. Try to be positive. Nothing will be changed if you stay where you are. You should take a step forward. You should vote and make your vote counts. Hopefully this negative attitude will not hold the same amount of negativity that happened in 2004.

I hope people will do something to change the current horrible situations. The terrible and intolerant situations that are gathered during the eight years of President George W. Bush and his administration changed the history of the world to the worst. I do not know if the world will ever come back as before the era of the second Bush. I hope it does. However, this will not happen by chance or by our good wishes. We have to be realistic. We have to think about the current miserable situations, which we all wish to turn into a positive future. People cannot just wait and say they were waiting to give the leaders a chance to change their way, attitude, or behavior. Don't be like the chance giver.

THE CHANCE GIVER

*D*o you know who the chance giver is? Take a guess. He is the one who said he stayed in the White House to give the president a chance to change the lies he said. Ha! Ha! Ha! Please guys, join me and let's enjoy this joke. Do you know him now? He is Mr. Scott McClellan, the former White House Press Secretary and the author of **What Happened?**

How wonderful is that to come now and say in many TV interviews, including the one with Fox News' Bill O' Reilly that he did not know at first what he was saying in his press conferences was false. He added he knew after that but he stayed in his position and kept telling the lies of the Bush administration, which he was one of its important members and figures, to give the president a chance to correct his position.

Thanks a lot Mr. McClellan. Do you think we did not know that you were both lying to the world? You were the front of this administration that represented them and their lies. You are not convincing at all. What made you wake up now and say the president was lying? Did you have a dream that made you come back to your conscious and thoughtfulness? Perhaps, you can give us a better explanation Mr. McClellan.

Now, and according to your great story, you gave the president a chance. Did he change his position, his explanations about his glorious war towards Iraq, or about the young men and women he put in harms way? Do you think your book at this time was going to make him do something good or admit his mistakes? You were part of the worst administration in history Mr. McClellan.

Mr. McClellan! Look at the general attitude of the people now. You will find out they are not satisfied with you, the president, the vice president, or the whole administration. Thanks anyway for the good lip service you gave us lately about you, your book, your position, and your feelings at this time. We can do nothing but thank you hundreds of times man, Kudos to you Mr. McClellan.

Senator John McCain

Senator John McCain could have done a very much better job if he had not been supported every word, action, and decision of President George W. Bush. Senator McCain caused himself great damage by just following the president, no matter he was right or wrong. In fact, this continual support might show fatal results during the coming presidential elections for Senator John McCain.

Senator McCain is expected to be leading the same way as this current administration. He says he is different but it is hard to say even any slight difference. He acts, talks, and gives remarks about any issue the same way. For example, his statement about Iran is very much similar to the statements of the president and the vice president. He is an obedient student for the administration, helps serving their wicked policies. He wants to stay in Iraq for another 100 years.

Let's go back to the gas issue. Senator McCain, by staying in Iraq for a hundred years, will double and may treble the current gas and food prices. Just remember with me when the gas prices reached $2.00. How everyone was upset about that unreasonable price? See how this administration is fooling everyone. They made us now run to any gas station which sells gas for just $4.15 to $4.25 saying and believing this a very cheap and fair price. Look how their policy is; increasing the prices every single day. Did any of us imagine we will be paying these huge amounts for gas? Did any of us think a hundred dollar bill was not going to fill up his or her small gas tank? How in the world simple and poor people can lead their lives? Do you see how all these miserable situations are gathered?

Senator McCain
and the New Car Battery

Senator McCain says he is going to have some genius people invent a different new car battery. He promises people with many things, saying the new batteries will be invented because he offers a fair price which is a dollar from every American. Inventions were not invented this way senator. I agree with you that many inventors and talented people are Americans. Nobody can deny that. People do not invent because someone seduces them with money. They invent because they are able to, and because they have a gift from God, not everyone can have.

People do not want any more dreams senator. People need reality. People can enjoy dreaming but then they wake up finding themselves stumbling. This is already the case with the current administration. Look how people's dreams and belief in false promises took them in a blocked way. People are fighting others who are suffering like them because they once believed promises like yours. I think people should have learned their lessons and therefore, it should be hard for them to be fooled again. The damage occurred by this administration leaves no room for any more fooling or deception. It might not be deception but promises based on dreams and wishes can do people no good at all.

Do you remember senator when people used to think about invading other planets and creating a new life there? How many decades ago people talked about such flourishing dreams? What did people achieve from those dreams? They achieved nothing and nothing at all senator. You should have a better plan if you want to persuade people with what you say.

You have said, "Do you remember how much people used to pay for cell phones when they were first invented? They used to pay about $1000.00. Nowadays, people get them for free." Senator! What do you mean by that? Are you going to give people stuff for free? I hope so. Tell me what is for free now? Some elderly folks used to say, "There is nothing for free, except for deafness and blindness." God forbids, we do not wish those two things for anyone.

Senator! you remind me with those commercial letters that used to come by mail, and are still coming so far, asking people to subscribe for a magazine or whatever issue, in order to win millions of dollars. We used to get fooled by those things. I hope the number of people who still believe in such deceptions is decreasing. We need to live the reality. We do not want to be dreaming for the rest of our lives.

Senator! You should help dissolving the bad gathered situations, which are resulted form the administration you support. Such dissolving and examination can occur only through careful studies, considerate feasibility studies, and real experts' opinions. You say you can imitate the Brazilian experience of using octane in order to solve and decrease the American problems of consuming gas. Why are you so sure you will and you can do it? It has been so many years since it happened in

Brazil and people here already thought about it and tried to imitate it but they could not.

How long will that issue take to do? Are you going to use your magic wand to achieve it? Be careful senator about the statements you make and do not be like the current administration. I hope this is not like the ***mission accomplished*** statements and promises. Look how many years have passed since we read that mission accomplished sign behind the president in that warship when he delivered his speech. The mission had never been accomplished and the proof is your wish to stay in Iraq for 100 years senator. I hope your battery and octane solutions you are promising the people at the moment are not in your same 100 year plan. This means the mission will not be accomplished during the life of any human or creature on the face of the earth now, except for very few ones, of course.

CREATING JOBS

I do not know again what people should do to have a job that matches their schooling and majors. People are experiencing a great deal of hardships more than any other times. Let me talk about myself again, just to clarify the picture, and nothing more. I might be different but there are many Americans who can hardly make a decent living at this moment.

Let me start with my situation first. I mentioned before that the very best job I could get was a substitute teacher. I explained as well, how that kind of job causes the substitutes headaches and pains beyond toleration. I applied for other regular educational and non-educational jobs. All what I got was either in fast food restaurants or gas stations. Thank God for finding a job, of course. My case is very much better than those who cannot find one. It is also better than those who live their lives begging and wandering the streets and stores explaining their hard situations to others in order to give them a dollar or two.

I applied for the cruise ship job in Hawaii in 2006. If you have read my previous book, *Leave People Alone*, you must know a great deal by now about me, my personal and practical life. During the interview, which I went to with my dear friend Douglas Logwood, the lady interviewer asked me about my qualifications and work experiences. I showed her my certificates and everything. She explained to me later that the jobs they can offer me are either room services or kitchen jobs. I chose the room service.

After finishing the medical exam and all the requirements for that job, I got a call from the people in charge of that cruise company telling me if I still want to go, the only job they can offer me is a dishwasher. They waited until I had told the people I work for that I was traveling to Hawaii. Everyone I know knew that already. The business owners of my job found a substitute for me and set a day for him to start working. Tell me guys what I could do then and what you were going to do if you were in my position.

After lots of thinking and consideration, I decided to go. I had no other choice. While being there, I remembered something very important. When the interviewer asked me about my cooking experiences, I told here that I worked as a pizza manager and cook and I was also a crew leader at Wendy's. At the same time, I was a cook and a cashier there. She did not find me sufficient for such kind of jobs because of her valuable offer. While being in the ship one day doing some cleaning, I was told to go inside the pizza shop and clean it.

Let me explain more: They call dishwashers a "Utility Galley." This utility galley includes all kinds of washing dishes, cleaning, sweeping, and mopping. The first offer in my first contract was a "night cleaner." The only thing I liked about that job was that I could go out in the daytime and watch the different beaches and beautiful sites of the Hawaiian Islands. The times I got a chance to do that could be counted on the fingers of my both hands. I could not do that very often due to my schooling and studies. I could hardly sleep. They never allowed us a day off for any reason.

When I was told to clean the pizza store, I asked the girl who was working inside if she had any experience with pizza. She told me she did not have any but they gave it to her. All what she had to do was to put the items on the pizzas, put the pizzas in the oven, and take them out. What a beautiful job! I wondered and asked her about the reason my interviewer did not give me such a job although I told her about my experience with pizza. I did not tell her about my cleaning experiences although I had many. This is because the business owners usually use their workers' situations. When they know that the person is in need of the job, most of them act nastier and meaner.

Moreover, I found out the ship has a centre for children. They said people must have a bachelor's degree to work in such a center. I had a master's degree in Children's Literature and am working on my doctorate degree in education. Why couldn't I get such a job? I did my very best, my friends, to change my job and bad gathered situations but in vain. Do you think I could have done any more? In fact, I did.\

After inquiring, trying, and requesting, I was told I can change my job any time and I just have to reapply for the job I wanted. I reapplied about five times. None of those applications made me any difference. Let me tell you about that nice incident. I was told that my department manager should have to sign the application in order to be approved. I found out, my friends, I am wasting my time, effort, and consuming myself at the very time I needed to use that effort studying or sleeping.

Ronald, my department manager took more than one application from me. He neither signed them nor gave them back to me to take to the human resources (HR). He kept them and told me he was going to give them to the HR manager himself. I kept waiting and waiting with no answers or responses. One day, I went back to Ronald asking him what happened with my applications. Ronald assured me he already gave them to the human resources. I waited for another couple of months and then went to the HR manager who checked on his computer and assured me that Ronald had never given them any of my applications.

Had you read my other book ***Leave People Alone***, you should have known about my other experience about the school assignment and how I had to meet a school or a university leader to write a paper about such a meeting and interview. I have mentioned that I met a nice lady named Suzette Robinson who was a leader in Maui Community College and how another lady in Hawaii University gave me an appointment and then changed her mind and let me down.

For that paper, it was recommended to have more than one interview. I explained what happened to me to Ronald who showed a great deal of rejection to what happened and sympathized with me. He knew about the hard situation I was experiencing; being in a cruise ship that moved from an island to another almost every day and being a doctoral student who needs to do lots of assignments and writes too many papers at the same time.

Of course, all that was before the applications of changing jobs. Ronald told me then that he knew a school principal who was a close relative to him and he was going to take me to him one of the Sundays while the ship ported in Honolulu, Ronald's hometown. We both agreed it did not necessarily have to be a school meeting as his relative; the school principal could have an interview with me and explain his leadership styles anywhere. Two months had passed after that discussion. Ronald saw me every Sunday night and told me, "I am sorry man. I did not go out today. I did not see my relative or talk to him. We will do it next week. I promise." I already gave up after the third time he told me that same story. I just listened and let him finish whatever he had to say.

The point I am trying to reach here is how things are deteriorating. Consider how many other people have to handle similar or worse situation because of the very bad life conditions we are experiencing at the moment. Look how our bad situations are gathered and accumulated over us. We have to be either strong or collapse. We do not have much choice. We see people take advantage of us, use our circumstances very badly and we still have to be obedient. What is the end of all that? Only God knows. ***God helps us. We suffer.***

OTHER CRUISE SHIP STORIES

Back to the cruise ship; let me remind you if you have read my previous book with Charles my direct boss and Ronald, our general manager. Charles told me, after the great lecture and demonstration, he gave me in front of the other workers in his very loud voice that he had an hour and half meeting, just about me, with Ronald. He said they were discussing how slow I was at work. Charles used to say I am his best and fastest worker. He said many times before that he was so proud of me. Charles changed 180 degrees after I refused his lousy racist remarks and stupid jokes about Arabs being terrorists and exploders. See how people can become very mean!

When things deteriorated between me and Charles, they moved me to work on a different deck, same kind of job, night cleaning. It was a little better to stay away from Charles and his lousy jokes and remarks. However, I had to deal with Greg, his dear friend, who took over giving me lectures and demonstrations on how to be an excellent cleaner who cleans properly and smoothly. I had no choice, either to resign from the ship then, or listen to Greg. Greg was sometimes nice. I trusted him and thought he acted that way maybe because they told him he was my boss although he was not a manager. Greg was just a galley steward (GA).

Some of the guys who took that remarkable rank (GA) became very proud. You could feel that they spoke from their nose as a sign of pride. The GA issue takes me back to Ronald who once later told us he was going to promote many people to GA. He almost promoted all the lazy workers who are good at the lip service. He left hard workers without promotion. I remember Herbert, my former roommate in the ship when he came to me sad, telling me we both did not get the GA promotion like the rest. In fact, GA is nothing. We just wanted to know how much they appreciated us. We both found out that their amount of appreciation towards us was zero.

Back to Greg and his trust, I tolerated him and did whatever he told me to do. However, many times, I felt what he was telling and ordering me was recommendations from his very dear friend, Charles. That trust continued until one night when I arrived at my working station with Greg, Greg handed me an official note from our department ordering me to go to work in a different station in our deck which was, "The Hot Pot Wash."

If you are not familiar with The Hot Pot Wash, please allow me to explain it to you. It is the station where they wash all the large pans and any pots, mostly the large ones that do not fit to be placed in the dishwasher machine. Therefore, the dishwasher's job, according to too many workers, is a lot nicer and more decent than the hot pot washer. The hot pot washer has to do everything manually. In addition to that, he has to remove all that food remains in the trays the cooks come and threw to him, especially if he does not have a chance to tell every cook to remove the food remains left in the trays and pans they bring him. It is also recommended that the hot pot washer should be a strong one with big muscles so he can handle lifting those heavy pans. He has to be very careful too as many of them burn their hands and arms in the hot water as the water in their sinks has to be boiling. In addition to that, the hot pot washer has to pay a great deal of attention and look around him all the time. Some of the trays he washes have sharp edges that can cut his hands like a knife. If the cooks placed them in one of the top shelves in a wrong way, one of those trays with sharp edges might fall over the washer's face, neck, or head and you can imagine the conclusions.

Consider all that. That is why many people believed being workers in the hot pot wash station was a punishment. I did not say anything. I went to that station, where I started my real friendship with my dear Nigerian friend, Daniel. Daniel was a GA but he is a nice guy. He was a very hard worker too. Daniel told me about his sufferings in that ship as well as others and how he was promised years ago to be promoted but never got that promised promotion. He was a GA for years but you already know my friends, how many people in charge promote those who do nothing in their jobs and leave hard workers. They have a point here. Their point is if you promote a good worker and make him or her a manager, you will lose the valuable services he or she does to you. Then, you have to look for another hard worker and you can hardly have any guarantees you will find him or her. How fair is that?!

Do you agree with me such kind of bosses and managers can discourage hard workers and create a negative attitude? Who has set the regulation, which says the good people are to be taken advantage of and the lousy ones are to be promoted and taken very good care of? Why do people always imitate the bad behavior? Why do many people like to disappoint the good and honest people?

I know that people should treat others the way they like to be treated. Is it racism, lack or respect and appreciation, or revenge for whatever reason, what is it? I hope I know one day and give you the answer. Honest and hard working people need to know what they can do to satisfy others, to feel appreciated, to give more and more efforts, sincerity, and honesty.

That is why the majority of people wish to have a better future in spite of the terrible economy crisis we experience, which politicians and economists call a recession. The recession has taken so long and it is getting worse every day at the expense of good people's nerves and feelings. What can people do to improve their situations if they do not want to steal, rob, and kill to get whatever they want? Those honest people need real and quick solutions. People do not need promises nobody knows any of them will be achieved or not. They need something fast, faster than that chargeable car and new battery.

LACK OF BALANCE

Nowadays, I feel that people are losing their sense of balance. They do not know how to measure the estimation and appreciation towards others. Going back to the cruise ship, why does a hot pot washer, a cleaner, or a dishwasher work a lot harder than all the others and get paid less than everyone else? Where is justice here? Those are human beings too. They spare no effort to make the working conditions and place very much better. Where is your appreciation and support?

The lack of balance also leads me to another issue, which is the lack of honesty and integrity. We were all told during the interview before joining the cruise ship that everyone gets paid the same which as they said then was $6.50 per hour. We later found out that all those were just a bunch of lies. The ship jobs are different and the Utility Galley people receive the least and worst payment.

I believe the Utility Galley workers should be paid, at least, the same amount like waiters and room service staff, if not more because of their hard work, the dangers they face in their jobs, and the mental and physical stress they had to go through due to some of their bosses and managers' lousy treatment. If not, they should not blame the utility galley staff then if they do not work as hard as they expect them to do. Those people are not machines. They are people like you. It is not fair to find a manager like Charles showing up at the beginning of every night and then once again around 5.00 a.m. pretending to be mopping the galley. That is kind of smart as he used to choose the time when most of the cooks leave or arrive at their working stations so they all see how a hard worker he was. What a hard worker who slept day and night and worked five to ten minutes then gave another excellent lip service in front of all the people there to be a good boss.

Moreover, let me explain that a great deal of waiters and cooks deal with the utility galley people as if they were their slaves, especially the cooks. I am not against anybody but I am just telling you about some of the experiences that happened to me and other co-workers, which I had seen and watched with my own eyes. For example, most of the cooks come and threw their dirty pans to the hot pot washer and got so angry at him, giving him lectures if, according to them, the pans and the trays, were not arranged and organized properly so they can pick them up very quickly.

That is why I do not also blame some of those galley people when they show a bad attitude sometimes. Do you remember the pizza girl I told you about? One day, Daniel, my former co-worker in the hot pot station was in his vacation. I had another co-worker named Dennis. The pizza girl named Kathy came to our station saying hello. Dennis frowned and said to her, "Don't you have anything to do?" The girl said, "No." She added she was not that busy and she just wanted to greet us. Dennis and I laughed at that situation later but we did not laugh when it occurred.

Dennis acted that way because he felt it was unfair we were working hard while others were having a lot of free time and were just wandering around us to say hi. The point here is to show the unfairness and dissatisfaction some people might feel. This leads to other bad feelings like discrimination and injustice.

I know the pizza girl, Kathy is very nice. She did not mean to show either of us any of the above feelings. The people in charge create aggression between people. This worsens relationships and friendships. Some people might take it personally and get offended, thinking others are either taking advantage of them because of their race, color, religion, or ethnicity. All this takes America back to the age of racial discrimination. These issues should be avoided, especially at this time. People are losing their patience because of their financial suffering. Such suffering is more than enough for all of us. Nobody needs another person to look down on him or her.

The top administration should set a good example by showing people it does not discriminate. I think many people can tell the Bush administration is careless about not showing discrimination and double standards. The administration's reaction after Hurricane Katrina is one of the clearest examples about that.

Let's go back together and remember when President Bill Clinton said the Bush administration wanted to give him tax exemption, which he believed not to be right. He is considerate and knows well there are poor people who suffer and need that exemption more than him. Look at the former president's two terms and see how people were happier. Nowadays, people almost forgot how to smile.

Let's also remember together the four years of President Jimmy Carter's presidency. I know you might tell me there are many critics for the former president. Please, do not just look at one incident and forget about all the achievements President Carter had done. Don't forget nobody is perfect either. I once read that Secretary Condoleezza Rice was a democrat then she shifted to the Republican Party. She did not approve the way President Carter dealt with the American hostages' crisis. Would she have been satisfied if he had bombed Tehran? I can tell the answer now from the way she deals with the world and her enthusiasm for bombing Afghanistan and Iraq.

Secretary Rice! Do you still see the way President Carter dealt with that crisis was wrong? I can assure you still do but you are wrong. Don't you think if he had bombed Tehran then, he would have created too many more enemies and terrorists? Don't you know obsessive use of power and aggression creates more violence, disrespect, and hatred?

Iran and Palestine

Look how President Bush and his administration have been dealing with the Middle East crisis. President Bush followed the steps of Ariel Sharon, the former Israeli Prime Minister. He said, "Sharon is a man of peace." For God's sake, who is a man of war then?! Who can remember a single peaceful act for Ariel Sharon? Sharon has been famous of his brutality all his life. He always had a blood thrust, which was never fulfilled or satisfied.

President Bush dealt with the late Palestinian president exactly like Sharon. I know a good leader should always give the other person at least one chance and try talking with him himself, not relying on what others said. That should have happened before considering Yasser Arafat a terrorist. Let me say and assure you that Arafat was more than patient with Bush and Sharon. I cannot imagine any other person in Arafat's position would have been so patient handling all that disrespect from both leaders.

The two leaders; Bush and Sharon, assumed Arafat to be the reason behind all the violence and lack of stability. They also said many times that conditions would be much better without Arafat. Please tell me if that had happened After Arafat's death. Your opinion here is like that of my friend, Dr. John Green. He told me once that Arafat was a real terrorist. I was surprised by his remark and he wondered why. He talked as if he was stating a fact.

John! Allow me to ask you now why do you think so. Why do you sometimes think others who disagree with you to be naïve? I do not want to say "idiots." This is really the way you sound sometimes.

Let's move to Iran and its nuclear problem. Why does this administration refuse negotiations? What did it reach with any party? I used to have an Iranian friend named Reda. One day I asked him how his weekend was. Reda said to me, "I cannot enjoy a weekend. People always see me here as a terrorist." Don't you agree with me that this administration has a great deal to do with that? Do you see how the wrong practices of this administration create distances and gaps towards people of color, race, different religions, or ethnicity?

In a recent TV program, I watched a group of Americans who visited Iran and were happy with their visit. They found out the Iranians they met there are nicer than they have ever imagined. Another question is sticking to my mind here. Please, allow me to ask it. If a person like Reda encountered a bad experience in America like the one I just told you about, can we blame him if he goes back to Iran and avoid Americans there or acted rudely with them? I am against rudeness anyway. However, if you can find yourselves excuses, why do you refuse to give others the same excuses? I can also see how things got bad with this administration, which gathered all the bad situations. These bad situations became harmful to America and the rest of the world.

Let's draw a comparison between the Bush presidency and administration and the presidency and administration of President Jimmy Carter who succeeded gathering the late Egyptian president,

Anwar Sadat and the late Israeli Prime Minister Menachem Begin. President Carter is still working to spread peace and stability on earth until now. Go back to the year 1977 and see his achievement of making peace between Egypt and Israel. I remember how every Egyptian was proud of President Carter. Can you see the big difference between President Bush and President Carter and the two administrations?

President Carter gathered other leaders for peace and stability while President Bush gathered them for war and destruction. Let's also go back again and remember the hypocrisy of Mr. Scott McClellan who is pretending now he had not known about the Bush administration's lies and misleading. How should people feel when they watch a good and excellent speaker like Mr. McClellan talks with great confidence and enthusiasm about the validity of the Bush administration's policies and war then comes now to tell us he did not know about their deception?

Does he think the whole world to be naïve to tell us he was giving President Bush a chance to correct himself? Correcting his position in what: Killing and destruction? You already had given him many chances to spread all the inhumane conditions and situations and to defy the whole world.

Mr. McClellan! Look at your administration's practices and how they still put President Nelson Mandela's name in the list of terrorists who are not allowed to enter the U.S. President Mandela then was not wrong when he had said President Bush and his administration are defying the whole world represented by the United Nations because it was led by a black man, hinting to Koffi Anan then.

Do you understand the point that this administration's practices are imitated by many individuals? For instance, if we see the cruise ship as a small republic, don't you think people of color, religion, and other races can feel they are ignored, insulted, and humiliated like the way President Mandela felt after the beginning of the war against Iraq.

Many people take their leaders as an example. Some of them might think mean and reckless actions are good because they are practiced and imposed by their leaders. I do not want to repeat myself here. If you had read **Leave People Alone**, you already know how many insults I had experienced while being in that cruise ship. A majority takes it for granted that the people of the Middle East are terrorists who should not be hired in cruise ships because they are going to explode them. Situations are gathered here by this administration against the people of the Middle East. What do you expect if President Bush announced he was going on his crusades towards these people? Others might act as crusaders too in order to protect themselves from those dangerous people. Who is the first person to be blamed her?!

President Bush once announced he is the "decider." Hence, he decided Arabs are bad. He also wondered, "Why do they hate us?" Most of the people since then had taken it for granted that Arabs and Muslims hate Americans and spare no effort to attack and kill them. Consider this classification. Is it a good one? Do you expect people to be happy and appreciate you when you say they are terrorists? They do not hate you guys. They hate this administration, which spares no effort to dehumanize them and turn the rest of the world against this part of the world. Situations here are completely gathered against the Middle East.

SENATOR BARACK OBAMA

The way the media talks about Senator Barack Obama is very insulting when they wonder, "Is Senator Obama a Muslim?" Of course, Senator Obama and the media have the right to talk about his religion. Asking the question about the senator's religion should not be asked in a manner that supports the bad propaganda about Islam and the stereotypical issue that pretends Muslims are terrorists. This is absolutely wrong. Islam is a religion of peace, which rejects violence, destruction, discrimination, aggression, terrorism, and all kinds of cruelty. Why do you ask the question in a bad manner? You should not act like those who always like to show themselves as enemies of Islam and Muslims. Such people act like that ship leader who was happy to fire six Yemenis from the ship.

Back to Senator Obama, I am really glad because he had apologized to those two Muslim ladies of Dear Born who were forbidden from sitting behind him in order not to be seen on TV. I believe Senator Obama when he said he had not known that and he would not have permitted it in case he was asked. Senator Obama is helping dissolving the bad gathered situations created and promoted by President George W. Bush and his administration, which they aimed at Arabs and Muslims.

Consider the last New Yorker's magazine cartoon about Barack and Michelle Obama. What do those artists want? It is obvious they are trying to turn Senator Obama the way President Bush is. They want Obama to be an enemy of Islam and Muslims. They scare him in order not to be nice to anything concerning Muslims. They want to worsen the relationships between Americans and Arabs, which are already worse than anyone could have ever imagined some years ago. The way the New Yorker acts is exactly like the way haters act. They want people to live in disputes, aggression, and conflicts. No matter whether they tell us they meant it this way or a different one. Again, such practices are an offense to every single Muslim all over the world.

FOREIGN POLICY

My friend John Green told me many times that I do not know about foreign policy and I should just talk about things I understand. You might be right, Dr. John. I am not a politician but I know about human relationships and their importance. I believe everything starts with a human relationship. We cannot live without other people as it is a cycle as everyone relies on others for a certain reason or need. That is why I am in the favor of the advice that you should not spoil your relationship with anyone you know as you might need him or her one day. Unlike Senator Obama, there are many people whose main concern is to insult others, especially Muslims and Arabs. I wonder again why those people who do not show even little respect cannot leave people alone.

Aggressiveness and Hatred

*D*o you remember the former presidential republican candidate who said he was ready to bomb Makah and other religious Islamic places in case he was elected president? Now, I tell him: There is no wonder sir that you were kicked out of the presidential race very quickly. The world does need not you or your valuable services. The world needs peace makers and not war mongers like you. Sir, you have to know that Muslims have no joke about their sacred places. You did an excellent lip service then you were gone forever. I congratulate the whole world for your failure.

People like you can cause a third world war. I am certain you do not care about the damage and destruction that would happen in case of having a president like you. You think you would be protecting America but such a policy or even talk proves you know nothing about protection or even politics. You thought people were going to applaud to you and support the trivialities you tried to spread but people are already fed up from people like you and cannot wait for a better change. You need to leave people alone and mind your own business. If your business is giving a lip service, you can talk about something else that might be helpful to you and your community.

You thought you were going to be the next world leader. Look where you are now. You almost disappeared. I see you as an invisible person and that is why I am glad I do not listen to your fantasies and dreams of being another Victorian and warrior at such a time that needs peacemakers everywhere.

THE PROTECTOR

Like the previous protector, there is another protector from Texas who shot and murdered two Hispanics because he saw them in his neighbor's property. How in the world did you know they were stealing? I ask my friend John Green if he is reading this to be patient with me because I know him as a friend and a critic of me all the time for whatever I say or do.

I heard that Texas man conversation with the police dispatcher on TV. The dispatcher begged him many times not to shoot but the man has a blood thrust, which he wanted to satisfy and quench. I am not contradicting myself here. I am saying that because I know some of the readers might think so because of what I had mentioned before about those two men who attacked me in the gas station, those two cowards with masks and a gun. There are many cameras and video system in the gas station, and the police made a copy of that part of the tape that shows how they entered and how I was threatened and assaulted. Therefore, Mr. Texan, if you were doing your job and got assaulted, I would not blame you. You were in the comfort of your house, you saw two foreigners, you wanted to satisfy your need killing two persons from other ethnicities you hate.

The human soul has to be respected sir. You are not the God who takes the soul and give it to people. We do not even have the right to kill a pet or an animal that does not hurt us. How in the world did you know they were thieves? Even if they were thieves, were they wearing masks or carrying guns like yours? If I were one of the jurors, I would have never acquitted you. You are a coward who committed a cowardly act. Your hands are blemished with the blood of people you have no evidence they stole or did anything wrong.

I know many people are going to have too many arguments about what I am saying. I know this is America, and rules are rules and have to be respected. Just put yourselves in the position of others. Do not always find yourselves excuses to hurt other people, which reached killing and losing human lives to say you are protecting yourselves. Do not always say you are protecting your countries from illegal aliens. Illegal aliens are human beings like you.

If you say these are the rules of the state of Texas, I respect the laws but I do not find it reasonable to shoot someone just because you do not know him or her and he walked in the property of your majesty. By saying that guys! Please, do not be offended as I am addressing that particular person who killed the two Hispanics. You and people like you unfortunately are spreading the bad picture many people already see America through at the moment. The administration as well as racist people like you, protector are damaging the beautiful image people had about America. They were not even in front of your house. You shot them in the back. Again, what a cowardly act by a coward person like you sir!

You are not different from the Texas bus driver who told me to get off his bus because I loaded my baggage in the bus he thinks he owns, which his daddy has bought for him. A racist is racist, no matter what you do or say. People like you and him see others who do not look like you as their slaves. Let me thank that bus driver because he did not take a gun out of his pocket and shot me too. Thanks Mr. Driver for not donating me life. I appreciate it Mr. Driver. Two cowards in two different situations, with no proof of any wrong doing. For you, Mr. Protector and Mr. Bus Driver, you are causing America in general, and the state of Texas in particular, to look very bad.

What makes it worse is that President George W. Bush was the governor of Texas. Many people all over the world already had the idea about Bush that he is a cowboy before and after becoming president. His wars and policies assured the validity of that picture. However, I like Texas and have dear friends from Texas, like my friend Steve Potthoff who had already invited me to visit and I want really to visit him sometime as he is an excellent friend. Please Steve, before my coming, write my a list of the things I do not know about the rules and regulations of the state of Texas so I do not encounter a situation like that of the bus driver, which made his Highness insult me so many times in front of all the passengers of the bus. I also have to be careful so I do not walk or drive if I do not really have to. I might get stranded in front of a house or so then get shot and killed.

If you say those two Hispanics are illegal aliens, you do not know their circumstances. If you had read my previous book titled Leave People Alone, you will find me saying we should not hurt people who did not hurt us. I also say it is the authorities' mission, not ours, to deal with an offender. You might have the right to kill if you are in real danger. That man called the police and they arrived shortly. He could have left those two individuals alone as he called the police who were going to deal with them and find out what they were doing there.

Let's go back to the issue of racism. I ask this man, if you travel to another country and any unexpected incident happens to you so you had to stop to seek help or ask for directions, is it alright that the people you stopped at their house shot you? Again, I repeat, Americans are highly respected everywhere but a number of them do not show the least respect towards others.

Your situations are different because you can travel to any other country in the world just with your passport without a visa. So I tell most of you that do not blame others because they do not have the same advantage like you. Do not also blame them because their countries respect you and let you in any time you want. Do not pretend that you deserve to be respected but others are not. All humans deserve to be respected. All souls have to be dignified, protected, and left alone if we do not want to help. Those illegal aliens might have to leave their countries because of a very bad need to help their children, parents or even themselves.

You did not try to see what they wanted sir. You did not let them live their lives which are owned by God, and only God, not you or any other human being. Congratulations protector. I am sorry that you have to spend your life free. You should have spent the rest of you life in jail or being executed like those two you executed yourself Mr. Coward. No matter what I say or repeat, a racist is a racist and coward is a coward, Mr. Coward. Situations are gathered here guys, and such situations are not improving the picture of Texas or America.

That killing by shooting two persons in their back is very bad. It is stabbing someone in the back, which is an act of treason and injustice. Again and unfortunately, many people find the American dream they have dreamed about for so long to be illusion. Look at foreigners in America and see how they work very hard to earn their living and accept anything they get and there is still no appreciation.

In addition to all that, we all know that many Americans are ashamed to do the kind of jobs illegal aliens do. Who is going to do such jobs then? These people are not taking your chances because the work they do is very important. If you decide to deport them all, look how the conclusions will be. To be realistic and practical, you can do your best to forbid other illegal aliens from entering the states but do not say you can or will get rid of all the ones who are already in the U.S. because there is no way to do it. In additions to that, the bad economy resulted from the Bush administration will be deteriorating more and more. First, it will be deteriorating more because of the huge number of tickets the government has to pay for to send all of these homes. Second, because the government has to take care of their children who will stay here since they are born in the states and are legal citizens. Third, because you will have to find Americans who are willing to do their jobs then will have to pay them a lot more than you are already paying those aliens?

I agree with Los Angeles mayor and always like his positions and statements. He lately said that the aliens who commit crimes must be followed and brought to justice. At the same time, he thinks the other aliens who work hard for a living should be helped to correct their situations and adjust their status. I agree with him completely. If those are not helped, at least they should be left alone as they suffer a great deal because of their harsh life circumstances, the hard work they do, and the fact that they are away from their homes and families. Don't think all this does not matter because they are illegal here. No, you are absolutely wrong.

There is an old saying which means or says, "Why do you have to deal with the bitter situations? The answer is: We had some issues and problems that are bitterer than these situations." Such a saying hints to the fact that if people are not suffering from severe circumstances, they will not endanger themselves and their lives, by leaving their loved ones to come and work in the worst kind of jobs anybody can ever have or do. Hence, it is not easy at all, as you might think, for immigrants including those who are living in the United States illegally to be insulted, humiliated, and get the lowest payment anyone can ever have.

Many American business owners have said frequently that those whom you call illegal are sparing no effort in the jobs they have. Some of them also said that Americans do not work the same way like them. I do not want to sound prejudiced but I am just saying things and statements I have heard from the media or persons I already met and dealt with. I worked with many Hispanics too. They are honestly the hardest workers I have ever seen, dealt, and worked with during all the years I had spent in the U.S. Therefore, it is good to overcome the contradictions that exist in the American society. It is also thoughtful to appreciate the service some foreigners do and know they are not slaves or beggars. They need more respect as they are honest and hard working people who help a great deal in building and constructing the American society of today.

THE GUANTANAMO BAY PRISON

At the time we need to be more realistic and stop the contradictions, the Bush administration is not satisfied with the Supreme Court ruling of giving the Guantanamo Bay detainees their simplest rights. That Guantanamo Bay prison or facility, or you can call it whatever you like, is a very notorious place. Such a place has worsened the picture of America everywhere. It made many people all over the world wonder how America, which used to be the land of liberties before the current president and administration took the lead, reached that extent of stepping over the human rights.

The only continual explanation this administration gives and repeats to an extent that made us learn it by heart exactly like our names, if not more, is that the Guantanamo detainees are dangerous. Many of those detainees were released because nothing was proved against them. For example, an Egyptian professor who was teaching Arabic in Pakistan was released after almost six years because he did not do anything wrong or commit any crime. His only crime was that he was working and living in Pakistan. What kind of crime is that? Is it a new classification of crimes? How should such a person feel if he was put in prison for six years, especially that one with the worst reputation of all jails, prisons, and detention facilities?! People need to be respected and given their rights to defend themselves.

The current White House Press Secretary came lately to announce that no one wants the people of AL Qaeda to be walking in the streets of Washington and America. The Supreme Court ruling says those prisoners have to be given some more human rights. What is the press secretary doing and saying here? Is she going to come later, like her predecessor Scott McClellan to say she did not know earlier about the lies and deceptions of the Bush administration or she knew but she was giving them a chance to correct themselves, their statements, and their situations?! Maybe, as everything is possible, especially in our current time.

At the time the administration should work hard to improve the bad picture it gained by this Guantanamo Bay and Abu Garib prison, it does the opposite. It rejects the highest court ruling as it had rejected the United Nations decisions and wishes earlier. This administration is simply defying and challenging every person, institution, leader, or country for just disagreeing with any of its positions. This administration is gathering the entire bad situations together, which leads to increasing the negative attitude about the United States.

Just consider how people all over the world used to see America and how they see it now. The administration says it tries to improve the American picture but had not shown any real action or intention to prove the validity of its real endeavors to do that. I think we all know that "actions speak louder than words." That is why we should see more than sweet word, sentences, and promises. We need, even once, to believe what they say. They had us used to their lies and fake good intentions.

The Bush continual rejection of giving the Guantanamo prisoners any of their simplest rights reminds me of what the former Defense Secretary, Donald Rumsfeld had said years ago about not giving any of the Iraq and Afghan captives of wars any rights because they were not members of an organized army. Rumsfeld was also defying the Geneva Convention and inventing new rules for him and the Bush administration.

Please, let's go back together and remember one of Rumsfeld's jokes about the war in Iraq. Do you remember when the TV showed us those actions of looting, especially from the ones of Baghdad National Museum? Did you see how Rumsfeld allowed thieves and robbers to go inside the museum and take everything? Shouldn't he have done his best to forbid such wicked actions? Was it alright to destroy the monuments of one of the greatest and oldest civilizations in the world? Look at his response when he was asked about that in one of his press conferences. He answered by a joke. He said it was just one man carrying a vase and the camera repeated the same scene for so many times, which made people believe too many vases had been stolen from the museum. Who in the world is Rumsfeld fooling?! Is joking and laughing are the ways to answer serious questions like that or is it just a practical and intelligent way to skip responding to harsh questions and get away with anything we do or commit?

I remember in one of the Larry King Live episodes, Larry King interviewed Donald Rumsfeld. The second night, he interviewed the Dixie Checks who opposed the war against Iraq. An audience called greeting them and Larry King and thanking them for taking the audiences' phone calls and answering their questions. The same audience said in his call that the Dixie Checks are brave because they were not afraid to take people's calls live unlike Rumsfeld who had his interview taped in advance and took no phone calls at all from anyone. I think we can tell he was avoiding embarrassment as he was going to receive many phone calls, which would have criticized him, his situations, his lies, and his role in starting that war.

I strongly believe people would have been much happier if he had worked for peace in spite of the fact that he was the defense secretary. That is why I have no wonder that many press agencies all over the world called him after the last two wars the American Minister of War and called the Bush administration the war administration. I even read more than once in an international newspaper that a certain writer called him President War Bush.

Do you remember the Sanford and Son Show when Redd Foxx used to say his name Fred J. Sanford, and every time he said the Letter J stands for something different? I think the W in the president's name can stands for War. Do you remember when the former Senator, Mr. Tom Daschle said he was very much disappointed with that president before that war erupted because we should save every single human life we can save, and not throw many lives and souls in harms way for no good reason?

The president defied everyone and went on his harms way, ignoring all the national and international calls and invitations to reconsider his position. However, there are some people who still support him and his position about the two wars and their necessities and urgencies. For instance, today I had a phone conversation with a dear friend of mine, Sarah Draper. Sarah told me she did not remember who she voted for in the last presidential elections. I told her that was not the thing that could be forgotten. She commented that when she said something she meant it and she did not lie. I know Sarah very well and I know it is not her habit to lie. Sarah told me she is not against President Bush but she is against those who supported him at the beginning and now are blaming and criticizing him.

Our phone conversation was interrupted for some reason so I could not respond to Sarah's comment. I tell you Sarah that, as I always repeat it, we are all humans, and therefore we are subjects to mistakes and deceptions. Those who supported the president and now are opposing him had not known his strong and glorious statements about the necessity, especially of the Iraq war, were built on lies. What can you say now Sarah about the former CIA director who came last year and told us that he had to lie because the vice president always told him to do that? What will you say about Scott McClellan who is telling us now the president was lying to the extent that he believed his own spin? What will you say about that? You do not have to agree with me about this issue or any other ones but I am trying to give you a sufficient explanation for what you are saying.

What can you say about the fact that this administration received a lot of information about some attacks that were going to happen before September 11 and did not share with public? There are too many things to think about before showing and expressing the strong defense you are giving President Bush and his administration.

Anyway Sarah, we are good friends and we have always differed with one another's opinions. However, this did not affect our friendship because we both know that everyone is entitled to his or her own opinion. We are not like this administration, which defies everyone who disagrees with it. We do not do like Vice President Dick Cheney who is famous for ridiculing and making fun of any of his own and his administration's critics. I have never seen him saying he made a mistake or he was ready to correct something he had said or done.

Just remember that America, which has the statue of liberty, should come back the way it was before, when it was the land of liberties. Nobody used to be scared or feel uncomfortable as people used to say. Look what is going on now. Most of the people are scared and worried.

People need relief. They need to feel secure about their current day and their tomorrow. You can hardly find people think hopefully like before. What have the innocent people done to experience all that? Maybe you can tell me. We have a common saying that "We are not going to fix the universe." However, our inquires and seeking for satisfying answers for the things that bother us can be of little help and hope of having a good tomorrow. I will not say a better tomorrow because I do not know when or how this is going to happen with all the current accumulated problems and bad gathered situations.

OTHER ISSUES IN
SARAH'S CONVERSATION

Sarah knew about the assault that occurred with me in my former midnight job in the gas station I worked for. I told her I feel like taking revenge from the individuals who attacked me. I do not have to do that myself but I will feel much better in case they get arrested. She wondered what good that would do me. I said at lease they were not going to do it with anyone else, which is good enough for me as I hate such cruelty and I do not want similar inhumane and cruel actions to happen to anybody.

During our conversation, I told Sarah about my feeling I discussed with you my dear readers before, which is imposing the death penalty in the State of Michigan. Sarah thought I meant that those two criminals and robbers should get the death sentences for robbing and assaulting me. I explained to her that I meant those two and others who commit crimes and murders like them would think one million time before attacking someone as I am sure they would have never hesitated to murder me if they failed to steal the money from the cash register drawer.

Sarah believed that the death penalty is a cruelty. I wondered if those two and people like them are not cruel. Had they thought it is alright for them to take the life of a human, why do we find it hard to have their lives taken? I do not say their lives should by taken by us of course but by the authorities after they are judged, given their chance to defend themselves, and also treated as "innocents until proven guilty."

Sarah! If you see death is cruelty and we should not say a killer should die. What about the innocents who were sent to death in the Iraq war? What guilt or cruelty had they done? Many American people who have lost a loved one do not feel the same way like you. Cindy Sheehan repeatedly said she supported the war against Iraq even after her son was killed until she knew he died while guarding an oil well. Can anyone bring him and others who were killed in that war like him back to life? Of course, we cannot.

You also disagree with me that imposing the death penalty will be a protection for society. I am making my point clearer again here by telling you I meant that will protect innocent people like you, me, and most of the people. At the same time, it will protect those bad persons who deviate from the right way. They will be scared because they know they will be dealt with very seriously in case of taking a human life as this life is not owned by them. They will know that every human life has to be respected. Again, as I had mentioned in an earlier chapter, if situations are stable in a certain state, it is up to the people in charge to impose the death penalty or not. If the crime and murder rates are beyond control, I think it wise then to impose such a proper punishment. Otherwise, things will continue deteriorating and good people will not feel safe or secure anymore.

I also think people now have more than enough to worry about. People are afraid of losing their houses if they have not already lost them. Therefore, they need to keep them or restart from the very beginning. Others think about how they will just pay the monthly rent and bills. People do not need any more worries or dangers in their lives. It is good that people can still handle all such cruel and harsh situations. It is more than enough for the people to handle all the bad situations, which are gathered on their way as obstacles, which need to be pushed away.

CONTROVERSY

It is not always bad to be controversial but it is very bad to be just controversial for the sake of controversy and stubbornness and nothing else. My friend John is over controversial with me to the extent that once he told me he had to work because he did not like what I was saying to him. Our conversation was about the war against Iraq and this administration. John insisted what is happening in Iraq was better and greater than what was happening during Saddam's era. John always told me to make my position clear but he never clarified his. As I had mentioned earlier, his best argument and advice for me is to just talk about what I know. John is almost telling me that I know nothing about anything at all in this life or world. I do not know why he thinks so or how he formed that opinion.

John did not like or appreciate my first book and that is up to him. I cannot force any friend, relative, or reader to like my book. I respect people's opinions. In addition, I know it is impossible to please or satisfy everyone. John told me that I do not mention in my first book *Leave People Alone* what and how Americans feel towards Arab. I tell you

John that I made my point very clear and said many Americans look at Arabs as terrorists. You also commented that I had not mentioned why Americans felt this way. I think I also made that very obvious and commented that many Americans like to see Arabs as the continual reason of their misery and unhappiness. John! Did you forget you had once told me that September 11 is more than enough to worsen the pictures of Arabs and make Americans hate them? Do you think you have the right to make statements such as this one and deprive me from my right to respond? I see your personal action here represented by many other Americans I have seen, known, and dealt with in my everyday life. However, I still respect and appreciate you and all the other persons who like to respond like you. I am not prejudiced against you or anybody as you might think. I love peace and unity. I feel my previous book and this one are invitations for love and harmony. I am inviting people all over the world to love and respect one another. I never make fun of anyone because of his or her opinions. I never stop anyone like you while making a statement and say to him or her, "Do not talk and listen to what I am saying." If I had interrupted you once or more, I was trying to investigate about something you had said or shown me. If I even have to interrupt anyone for some reason to add or clarify something, I do it with respect. I never intend to show that person anything other than appreciation, estimation, and consideration for the other opinion as I might learn something useful from him or her.

Another criticism you said John about **Leave People Alone** is that I said the American society does not accept for a man to have many sexual partners the same way it does not accept polygamy. Again John; I said it does not make sense when people with multiple sexual relationships that can produce many pregnancies and deliveries are left alone. They never care to see their children or the mothers of those children after that. They just think about a few minutes of sexual pleasure and then they are done with those ladies and their new born babies forever and they are not punished by the American laws for such a wicked action. Is it reasonable to leave those and go after a man who is married to more than one woman and who admits he is father of his own children and put him in prison? That is my point John and I cannot make it any clearer. I do not know how you think I had not clarified my points and myself enough. John! Your criticism and your way here do not assist your situation. I think I know and understand what I am talking about very well. Otherwise, I would have never talked about something I do not know the least about as you usually tend to say. Do you see how you are gathering and accumulating some of the negative things and attitudes about America and the American society? That is why I say situations are gathered from my conversations with you John and your opinions. It is not only our conversations, which helped gathering negative situations but you already know about too many negative things I experienced, which I mentioned in my two books as well as a great deal more of the other bad incidents I had never mentioned in them.

Negative Attitudes

former American friend of mine once told me to expect any wicked action and do not get offended or take it personally. That was in 2002, during the time we could still say people were still shocked and may have been excused for insulting and humiliating others who do not look like them. However, I have been here guys as you already know since 1998; a long time enough to know whether September 11 is the real reason or not. You might say I am repeating myself here. I am not repeating myself. The people who like insulting and humiliating others are the ones who are repeating themselves negatively and unwisely.

John, you travel to Egypt three times a year. You like it but you say people take advantage of you. I was told so many times; if I criticize some of the American actions I should go back home to Egypt. You told me that yourself. You once told me you did not like an action that happened to you when you stopped a man in Cairo to ask for directions. I told you then that man might not have understood you John. Had this man been rude and acted this way, should you judge a whole people of a nation because of him and his behavior? What about those three men whom I had told you about? To my dear readers, I was giving a ride to a colleague of mine to Detroit Metro Airport. On my way back, I got lost. I stopped at a convenience store, greeted three men who were inside there and asked them how I could go back to Ypsilanti. One of them said, "Ypsilanti! Let's see!" and then asked the other one, "Do you know Dave where is Ypsilanti?" The other said, "No, do you know Joe where it is? Can you send this man to Ypsilanti?" Then, all of them together laughed very loudly, "ha ha ha!" I looked at myself and my clothes to see what was funny. I could not see any strange thing in my appearance. I did not know why they laughed at me. I will not say they did not understand my accent because all of them repeated my question, which assure they understood my question very well. It was just difficult for their highness and brilliancy to treat me with respect, give me directions, or even say they had no idea how to go to Ypsilanti.

You tell me John that man you stopped in Cairo had not respected you. What should I say about those three men in Detroit who made fun of me for no reason except for passing time and having some fun? If you are always a very good critic of Arabs, aren't those Arabs entitled to defend themselves too? Are they just supposed to be listeners to you mocking them? How in the world do you think this can happen? John! That direction incident happened in the summer of 1999. Tell me it is also because of September 11.

Allow me please to clarify something. Those three men were White. I am not against Whites, Blacks, or Native Americans. I am just saying that to make it obvious that I am not racist. The guys who robbed me in the gas stations and assaulted me were Black. I want to clarify that I do not mean any offense here for African Americans. I will add that a White American also stole something from the same gas station when I was with Raed, my friend and co-worker. With the help of an African

American, Raed could go after this man and get the material he had stolen from the store in front of our eyes.

By mentionining colors, I am trying to tell you that I am not one of those racist people who criticize people for their colors. I do not just mention the negative things and leave the positives. It is not me and I will never be like that as long as I am alive. As I ended my previous book, I repeat it now: There are good and bad people all over the world.

Remember with me the cruise ship; I dealt with many good and bad people including Whites and Blacks. I am mentioning colors here because I do not think it is a shame to say a person is black or white although I never mention such labeling in my daily life. I remember my professor Dr. Gilbert Cross once mentioned to me and my colleges that there is no shame in saying Black when referring to Africans and African Americans. I had an African American colleague and another from Kenya who agreed with Dr. Cross as well as everyone else in that class.

I met some people who told me I am black and others who said I am white. In addition to those who said I am brown. I always answered that I do not care and it never bothered me at all to be called any of those. I usually said, "That is alright with me and I do not mind if that labeling satisfies you" and I always meant it. Why will we argue guys? Let's forget about these differences and argue about something more important. Let's argue about how we can improve our lives and conditions. Let's decide together what should be done and achieved to change the bad situations which are gathered against all of us. By continuing our controversy about race, we increase those bad situations. We are not helping at all.

ATTITUDE CHANGES

A colleague of mine in the merchant marine training facility and the cruise ship was very friendly. He always smiled to me as well as others whenever he saw me. We were almost friends but because of the different working shifts, we did not have a chance to have long conversations. I am not going to mention what color he is. I will say he is just American as I made my point obvious now and mentioned I experienced good and bad situations with different Americans of different colors. The same guy was sitting once with a group of his friends after they finished their dinner. I greeted them all but he did not return my greeting as usual. He also turned his face the other side. I thought if I had said or done anything wrong that made him upset. I could not recollect any thing of that kind. I came closer to him and said, "What is up man?" He looked at me and turned his face again. I said, "What is wrong?" He did not respond or look at me. How can you explain that?

Another day after that ignorance from such a colleague, we had a meeting with our general manager. The manager asked if anyone had any issue he or she wanted to raise or discuss. That guy raised his hand and told the general manager he had a complaint about one of his bosses and added, "We Americans like to be respected." I got a point from what he said and thought silently, "What about non-Americans? Don't they deserve respect and appreciation for their services too?" I began to find out that guy had a sudden change in his attitude. However, his sudden change gives me the impression that he is one of those racist people who might have thought I am American and changed his attitude towards me when he found out I am Egyptian.

I am telling that guy and people like him they should think about their actions and behavior. They should not make themselves judges and to judge themselves before judging others. They should be fair in their remarks and statements like my dear friend Kathleen Taylor who is an African American. Kathleen rejects any kind of violence or inappropriate behavior, no matter it is from Whites, Blacks, Arabs or whatsoever ethnicity.

I am now recollecting the famous speech of Dr. Martin Luther King in which he said, "I have a dream." I also have a dream Dr. King that everyone respects others. Unfortunately, many years had passed after your glorious speech Dr. King but many people cannot understand your speech and your dream. Unfortunately, many people, including some African Americans, do not appreciate other people who are non-Americans. Why do people like to degrade others? Why do many people like to invent and create problems with others without any reasons? Why can't those people leave other people alone if they cannot respect them? Dr. King! You and your colleagues had spared no effort to achieve unity and love. I do not think you could have done any better. You were murdered by a man full of hatred towards you and others who love everyone like you, Dr. King. We miss you very much Dr. King in the world of today. We miss you. Dr. King!

You and your friends have gathered your efforts to change the bad situations. Look at the current moment when people are gathering all the bad situations to achieve hatred and destruction. They feel they make glorious achievements by that at the time they offer the world more antagonism and dissatisfaction.

Confusion and Disapproval

.

I had mentioned in my first book ***Leave People Alone***, that a schoolmate of mine said he had taught his daughter to hate Arabs. This is not the only thing I am referring to now. I then wondered how it was possible to trust him when he was nice to me all the time during our class. Then, he suddenly said that shocking statement in my presence. This led me to think about other situations and how people can be double-faced sometimes and how to trust people who show us love, respect, and appreciation then suddenly shock us with an unexpected sentence like that.

Let me tell you about the landlord of my house and the other of a neighboring house during my early days here in Michigan. The two houses had a parking lot in the back, which seemed like just one spot. I always saw the boys and girls who live in the other house parking their cars in our space and never objected. One night, I was coming late from the school library around 2:15 a.m. I found a spot behind their house and that was the only available one. Just think about it. They left their cars for days sometimes when they traveled or had a friend who they shared a car with to save the gas expenses and that was alright. When I parked my car at 2:15 a.m. and went down at 6:30 a.m., my car was gone. The respectable landlord of the neighboring house saw me many times driving that car. It was too much for him to leave me a note on the car or knock at the door of the house, or ring the bell to tell me to move my car. He called a towing truck that came to tow my car. I ended up paying $155.00 for the towing company to get my car back. Look at the amount I paid for them for keeping my car in the towing company for about four or five hours in 1998, and my dear friend John Green still saying others take advantage of him. What was that John that happened to me? Don't you think that landlord and the owner of the towing company took advantage of me? Do you think it is that landlord's right to park his car behind the house I live in and do not allow me to do the same when I had too for a few hours in a snowy night? Where is the respect here? Where is the appreciation? I know Americans are practical and this is America. Just tell me John, why this practicality is not applied to them too?! Tell me why it is alright to accept any wicked action and bad behavior? Tell me what it means when I ask a neighbor to move his car from the driveway as I am late for work or a class and he tells me to hold on and keeps me waiting for about 20 minutes? Is this practicality or lack of respect towards others? Why don't you see such actions as rudeness and taking advantage of people too? Isn't this a double standard?

DOUBLE STANDARD

The Bush administration had increased the double standard nationally and internationally. They deal with different peoples with two standards. The wicked actions of some people against others, according to the Bush administration, are alright, as self-defense. When some others act the same way defending themselves, they are accused of terrorism, extremism, and aggression.

Like the Bush administration, many people are double standard. The former landlord of my house defended his friend, the other landlord and his action telling me it is their parking lot. What does it mean when that same other landlord and his tenants take my space and I complain to my landlord about that other landlord but he does nothing about it at all? Charles, my landlord always told me he would solve that problem immediately. He never solved it. Once again after my car got towed by the other dignified landlord, I never found a parking spot for my car. I had to call Charles. His wife answered many times and told me she could just tell him whenever he arrived. Charles answered once and advised me that I had to find myself a parking spot in our street or one of the neighboring streets? What a great advice!

Look at Charles and the Bush administration. See how the Bush administration advises some people to live in peace when they can hardly find food for their day. They ask people to be attacked and take it easy. They justify the wickedness of some people at the expense of some others. Good advice and excellent practice.

I want you to know guys, that was also before September 11. I had already mentioned it was in my first days in America. I am just reminding you because I know some readers might excuse such actions because of September 11. In addition to that, let's talk about Joshua who was my neighbor in the same house. Josh and I, as well as, two other neighbors were sharing one refrigerator the landlord placed in the kitchen. Joshua once left a dirty note to the three of us, his roommates who live in the other three rooms in the second floor, saying things I cannot write or mention here. It was, according to him and his note, because someone had eaten a piece of his cake. Another time, he left another similar note, because of a can of Pepsi or Coke. A few days later, Joshua knocked at my door asking me if I want his cake. I told him I did not want it. He said, "I am asking you because I am going to throw it away. Do you want it or not?" I said, "No. Go ahead and throw it away." How nice is that guys! Do you see any kind or respect in the way he offered me his cake?

Like Joshua, look again at the Bush administration and the double standard. Joshua was mean to me because I am not American and the other two were overweight. See how the Bush administration dealt with the people of Katrina in New Orleans. Look how they prefer some countries to others. Look how they talk about some with disrespect and show a great deal of respect towards others. I know my friend John will see the comparison here to be invalid but I see it to be very valid and sufficient Dr. John.

Another former friend was very nice until a certain time. She showed me how double standard she is. She once told me that, "We, especially those with blue eyes like me, have learned in good schools here in the United States. Others do not have what we have. We are used to a certain kind of life others do not know about." I never expected to hear such statements from her. I have nothing against blue, green, or colored eyes. I just again feel this is exactly very much similar to the discussion about color, race, and ethnicity, isn't it?

Although I do not like racism, I prefer the person who shows it to me in my face more than the one who shows me respect and stab me in the back. It is exactly like that Texas shooter who shot two Hispanics in their backs. Tell me what is the benefit of that Texas shooter in life and those people like him, if they have any? Maybe they think they have one, they think their benefit is that they think they are the only people who have the right to live and others should die or become their slaves if their generosity allows them to donate them some more years to live until they die or they decide to shoot them like the Texas Coward Executioner.

In our phone conversation, my friend Sarah had told me that nobody should take the life of anybody. Sarah! Do you think it was ok for that man to be forgiven? Don't you see how this encourages racist wicked acts like that? Don't tell me they were illegal here. If they were illegal in America, they still have the right to live their lives. The simplest rules of laws and human conventions say the defendants are "innocent until proven guilty." This coward shooter did not give them a chance to even move. He did not listen to the continual request from the 911 dispatcher not to shoot. He shot them. Should he be offered the Nobel Peace Prize for peace? You criticize other peoples and countries, Sarah, saying they shoot their people in the head. What do you say about the American who shot two people in their backs? At least the others you are talking about know in advance they are going to be shot. These two souls were taken suddenly and unwarily by a blemished blooded hand of a rude and wicked man. However, this was not an act of manhood at all. It was an act of treason by a person who knows nothing about the simplest human rights. Don't be double standard, Sarah, and see the whole picture inside America before you judge others.

Terrorism and its Origin

Let's try to think and speak wisely. Many people say that terrorism has an origin and always try to stick it to the Middle East. I tell you that you are absolutely wrong. Terrorism is everywhere and it does not have a home, religion, or culture. Don't just accuse people with everything and pretend that terrorism originated from a certain place and repeat stereotypical slogans and phrases others say. Let's remember together Yasser Arafat again and how he was always accused of terrorism by many Americans.

Yasser Arafat was seized inside his presidency building in Ram Allah, and his compound was hit by the Israeli artillery for many days. The surprise is to defend an American TV announcer blamed Arafat on a phone call while hearing all the bombing to his building with those who were seized with him for not stopping the violence. It was a natural reaction from Arafat to get angry and tell her to be fair as she hears the bombing and knows well he was seized in that building. Shouldn't people be reasonable guys before just throwing blames like that?

That announcer reminds me of some of the ship crew I had to see in my daily life on the cruise ship career. Some of them always found pleasure to let me hear their nasty statements about Arabs and Muslims. I used to tell myself then I am not going to have a fight with everyone as they might need me to do this. Therefore, they can say I am a real terrorist. How in the world they made themselves judges towards the peoples of many countries?! What are the qualifications that give them such a right?

Don't you remember Timothy McVeigh was American? Don't you also remember many others who committed terrorist acts were Americans? Let's not label people with brands like these. Let's remember together; no people of any country who are all good or all bad. Let's be realistic and stop that imagination. We cannot live with imagination. The fanaticizing we make just drives us backward. Let's not act or talk, like the Bush administration.

Concerning the Middle East problem, it is a very complicated one as all of us know. However, there was little hope for peace earlier but it died and disappeared with the beginning of the era of the Bush administration. Remember the people who worked for peace like President Carter and Clinton, President Sadat and Menachem Begin, and Yitzhak Rabin who was assassinated by an Israeli extremist who hates peace. We can describe the killer of Rabin as a terrorist. Rabin was a peace-maker and therefore he chose to kill him. This proves there are good and bad people anywhere on earth.

PEACE ON EARTH

chieving peace on earth is the responsibility of every individual. Had everyone started by fixing his character and behavior in dealing with others, peace will prevail. However, it is the major responsibility of the governments to make peace a reality, not just a dream. People are tired of dreams. There is hardly any more time to waste in dreams in our desperate era. We need more than dreams.

However, love and peace is my dream as I had mentioned earlier, that dream needs action from the people who lead us to become a reality. Peace should be achieved inside countries and nations. That is why those leaders should unite for that purpose. Law makers also should make and use sound judgments before imposing a law that says a house owner has the right to shoot people in his or her property. Where will peace come from then? The Middle East problem needs to be solved. Then, Palestinians and Israelis can respect one another and live in peace. This is the role of the leaders. Those leaders need to do something more than summits and conferences that support or reject and nothing happens after them. They need to think practically. This is the way, which enables them to overcome violence.

Let's go back a few years and see if the war against Iraq had not erupted, wouldn't situations have been better at the moment? Look how stubbornness can lead to deception to convince people of the right to do anything! Isn't that cruel? What did anyone get from that war other than destruction and disparity? See how the leaders gathered the worst situations that could have ever happened against all of us. Instead of working for people's welfare and happiness, they worked for their misery and sadness. Let's not be like those leaders and work for peace. We can, at least, achieve peace among ourselves by respecting one another. We cannot achieve happiness when we appreciate labeling people with nicknames and features we assume they have. Let's think more wisely. Let's improve our situations and circumstances. Let's dissolve the bad miserable situations imposed on us by bad administrations and governments. When those leaders know most of the people do not support their cruelty, they might reconsider and know it is good to be honest with their people and themselves, even once.

www.ingramcontent.com/pod-product-compliance
Lightning Source LLC
Chambersburg PA
CBHW020311290526
45784CB00003B/1465